The Story of Liberty
An American Symbol

Alison and Stephen Eldridge

Enslow Elementary
an imprint of
Enslow Publishers, Inc.
40 Industrial Road
Box 398
Berkeley Heights, NJ 07922
USA

http://www.enslow.com

Enslow Elementary, an imprint of Enslow Publishers, Inc.
Enslow Elementary® is a registered trademark of Enslow Publishers, Inc.

Copyright © 2012 by Enslow Publishers, Inc.
All rights reserved.

No part of this book may be reproduced by any means
without the written permission of the publisher.

Library of Congress Cataloging-in-Publication Data
Eldridge, Alison.
  The Statue of Liberty : an American symbol / by Alison and Stephen Eldridge.
    p. cm. — (All about American symbols)
  Includes index.
  Summary: "Discover what the Statue of Liberty symbolizes"—Provided by publisher.
  ISBN 978-0-7660-4061-8
  1. Statue of Liberty (New York, N.Y.)—Juvenile literature. 2. New York (N.Y.)—Buildings, structures, etc.—Juvenile literature. I. Eldridge, Stephen. II. Title.
  F128.64.L6E54 2013
  974.7'1—dc23

2011026430

Future editions:
Paperback ISBN 978-1-4664-0051-3
ePUB ISBN 978-1-4645-0958-2
PDF ISBN 978-1-4645-0958-9

Printed in China
012012 Leo Paper Group, Heshan City, Guangdong, China
10 9 8 7 6 5 4 3 2 1

To Our Readers: We have done our best to make sure all Internet Addresses in this book were active and appropriate when we went to press. However, the author and the publisher have no control over and assume no liability for the material available on those Internet sites or on other Web sites they may link to. Any comments or suggestions can be sent by e-mail to comments@enslow.com or to the address on the back cover.

Photo Credits: All photos by Shutterstock.com except p. 8, Library of Congress, Prints and Photographs.

Cover Photo: Shutterstock.com

Note to Parents and Teachers
Help pre-readers get a jump start on reading. These lively stories introduce simple concepts with repetition of words and short simple sentences. Photos and illustrations fill the pages with color and effectively enhance the text. Free Educator Guides are available for this series at www.enslow.com. Search for the *All About American Symbols* series name.

Contents

Words to Know 3
Story 5
Read More................. 24
Web Sites 24
Index 24

Words to Know

island　　　　**liberty**　　　　**statue**

I see the Statue of Liberty.

Liberty is a word that means free.

People in America are free.

The statue welcomes people to America.

The statue is a woman.

It is made of metal.

The statue is very big.

People are next to it.

See how small they look!

Where do I see the Statue of Liberty?

I see it on an island.

The island is near New York.

I see it from a boat.

Read More

Deady, Kathleen W. *The Statue of Liberty*. Mankato, Minn.: Bridgestone Books, 2002.

Drummond, Allan. *Liberty!* New York: Frances Foster Books, 2002.

Foran, Jill. *Statues and Monuments*. New York: Weigl Publishers, 2004.

Web Sites

NIEHS. *Give Me Your Tired, Your Poor* (The Statue of Liberty Song). <http://kids.niehs.nih.gov/lyrics/liberty.htm>

U.S. National Park Service. *Statue of Liberty National Monument – For Kids*. <http://www.nps.gov/stli/forkids>

Index

America, 5, 7, 9, 22
boat, 21
freedom, 7
island, 17, 19
liberty, 7
metal, 11
New York, 19
size, 13
torch, 13
welcome, 9
woman, 11

Guided Reading Level: B
Guided Reading Leveling System is based on the guidelines recommended by Fountas and Pinnell.

Word Count: 87